What Remains of a Life

poems by

Susan F. Blair

Finishing Line Press
Georgetown, Kentucky

What Remains of a Life

Copyright © 2018 by Susan Blair
ISBN 978-1-63534-447-9 First Edition
All rights reserved under International and Pan-American Copyright Conventions. No part of this book may be reproduced in any manner whatsoever without written permission from the publisher, except in the case of brief quotations embodied in critical articles and reviews.

ACKNOWLEDGMENTS

Publisher: Leah Maines
Editor: Christen Kincaid
Cover Art: Susan Blair
Author Photo: Tara Gimmer
Cover Design: Elizabeth Maines McCleavy

Printed in the USA on acid-free paper.
Order online: www.finishinglinepress.com
also available on amazon.com

Author inquiries and mail orders:
Finishing Line Press
P. O. Box 1626
Georgetown, Kentucky 40324
U. S. A.

Table of Contents

Storm 1

After the Dinner Date 2

For Anna, After Forty-Five Years 3

Old Poems for New 5

My Lesson 6

Mark at the Chevron Station 8

Linda Leaving 10

The Guilt of Innocents 12

Q.E.D. 13

Held 14

Harbinger 16

Greylock Bond 18

After Twenty Years 20

Sentinel 22

My Father's Hands 24

When You Pray 26

What Remains of a Life 28

Storm

The wind hurls water at the windows
like false accusations,
and shakes the power lines
senseless. I delay
my entry into this angry
morning, nestling deeper
under the covers. Why trek
through such wildness? Bed
is the best place to be.
The clock's digital face has gone
as blank as a sheet of rain;
the lack of juice at the switch
means a lack of coffee. Why rise
to such a brutal occasion?
Only folly, or fire, could shake me
loose from this nest. Here I am held
in warmth and ease,
here I am sure of my shelter.
Let the world rage
without me.

After the Dinner Date

Yes, you were young and alone
in the city, your new home,
craving companionship,
ready for romance.

Yes, he was German,
and to practice speaking it
meant a connection,
and soothed a kind of homesickness.

Yes, you yielded
to his persistence
and rode with him
on that dinner date.

Yes, you saw rape in the windshield
when he parked behind the warehouse
insisting that "*ein bisschen schmusen ist doch normal*,"
pulling you, pawing at you,

and yes, those bruises lasted a long time,
and you wanted to burn those clothes
and your teeth chattered
with the telling, with the reliving,

but ah, my dear child,
it's been a long time
and the woman we've become knows you spoke
the language of escape with your calm.

For Anna, After Forty-Five Years

In my dream last night
I was in your apartment
in Syracuse,
and you had died

a while ago, yet
I was there to check on things,
wondering why so much
was still there,

why the living room
was full of papers and books,
wondering at so much food
still in the fridge and freezer,

wondering at the basket
of cookies on the counter
and whether they were
the Ranger Cookies we baked together

when I got to spend the night
with you as a child,
finding a cupboard full of fine china
and wondering why this was still there,

finding the red table
where we played Go Fish
and Gin Rummy, where
you taught me how to play

Hangman and Scrabble,
and points of good grammar,
finding your organ in the corner
waiting for your expert touch,

remembering how you taught me
to play, and how, when you sang
Oh, the moon shines so bright
on Little Redwing,

the breezes sighing,
the night birds crying
in your strong soprano
I would cry,

and run to your bedroom
to hide my face in your pillow,
and I wonder now
what became of your violin

and why I can't remember
you playing it for me.
I wonder if you would smile
to have me discuss opera

and classical music with you,
if you would see yourself
in my obsession with good grammar,
and I wonder how, forty-five years

after your death, a dream
can make me miss you
so much,
Anna.

Old Poems for New

I pad through the bone yard
of discarded poems,
pawing through broken metaphors
and remnants of rhyme,
sniffing for a trace
of freshness
among the similes.
Mold and moss
drape the old thoughts;
the staleness
stifles.

I gasp for clarity.

Rummaging through forgotten
lines and verses,
I sift the shards
of literary ambition
for just one word worth salvaging.

This one, maybe.
Maybe this one can be revived.

A glimmer
among the refuse,
and I pounce.
The hunt has yielded
this gem:
"Hope is bone-deep."

I keep digging.

My Lesson

He swooped
from high above me,
folding his enormity
to hover
beside my five-year-old height
as I stood,
chalk in hand,
quailing.
The playroom blackboard,
beloved toy,
now leering blankly—
no game
this time.

Time for my lesson.

My father
had heard the cackles:
kindergarten valentines
all wrong.
He would catch
me, pounce
on my backwardness,
my mistake falling prey
to his love
for correcting.

Write the word "from."

His eagle eye would seize me
in my error,
snatch at the chance to devour my
wrong. I squirmed

in the trap, scrambled to formulate
an escape from the claws
of his criticism,
printed "F-O-R-M"
on the expectant blackboard.

A gleam in his eyes
a curl of his lip
a crow of triumph
at snaring my failing.

I saw the shape
outlined in chalk
his love for me would take.
His force would always be there
for me, to put my letters
to put me
in my place.

Mark at the Chevron Station
For Mark Hegge, d. June 2010

Small talk, that was all—
weather, wisecrackery,
the price of gasoline
rising again? What else is new.
What can we do
but drive on.
Banter about his stalled classic car—
a Chevy, of course—
hoisted high on the lift
in suspended animation
same as last time,
and the time before,
because repairs for pay
take priority.
I, anonymous, an occasional customer—
filling up now and then—
my face he knew:
"Hey you," his greeting.
"Mark" stitched on the right side
of his Chevron jacket,
the light in his eyes
reflecting his ease
and lightness of being.

The garage today, naked
without his classic Chevrolet—
I mark its customary spot.
Gliding down the street
at last? Shocks replaced,
transmission fixed?
Mark joy-riding?

The shock—
cardiac arrest.
At home, they said,
while watching the game.
The car at rest
in his driveway.

We were barely acquainted.
Yet I mark the presence
of his absence,
the hole in my life
his friendliness filled.
I gave him cash for gas,
he gave me reasons to smile.
I'd give him my hand now
to shake, say thanks
for the nice miles.

Then I'd drive on.

Linda Leaving
    for Linda Horsch, d. August 2011

What sparks that light
in her eyes the color
of alpine air?

She smiles easily
and finds reasons
to laugh at herself,
at life.

She is radiant,
though not, I am sure,
from the radiation, nor
from the chemo.

This one glows
from her own secret source
of insight, of fire and ice,
of love.

Her look promises
friendship, and I
fly to her gravity
like a wish to a star.

She waits at
that threshold, and
the door will soon open,
yet I dare –

yes! I dare! –

to stand
in her grace
and let it
shine through
the gaps in me,
to throw back
the flame
of hope. We lock
eyes on each other—

this, our secret
handshake.

She accepts my love
and I accept
her receipt of it,
both of us knowing
the price in pain.

The Guilt of Innocents

Disgust
shimmers around him
like waves of heat
rising from the desert floor,
shriveling our spirits
and drying the conversation
to dust.

Our time
had been safe,
I thought, but he
has turned his dark side
inside out again. Some word
was committed, or a look.
Our crime

will not be explained,
of course, but
punished. In the
searing silence
I learn to trust
in blame as his child
and await the blast that maims

from his furnace.

Q.E.D.

You turn over in sleep
and we are
face to face,
our pillows touching.

You breathe
cool puffs
over my cheeks
and eyelashes.

I lie
in the stream
of your life-force,
feeling the flow of you,
feeling your rhythm,
then turn over.

In sleep your hand finds
the center
of my back
and you press it,
spreading warmth.

Is there proof
in this connection?

Too soon
you turn over
again, leaving
a cold spot
where your hand
has been:

thus, our only
intimacy.

Held

Heard before seen,
that child.
From several yards away
I recognize the cry
of "I-am-fed-up-to-here-tired,"
which every woman can distinguish from
"I-am-hit-the-wall-hungry"
and "my anger-is-bigger-than-me."
A melt-down
as only an almost-three-year-old
can perform. I watch
the woman walk, turn,
coax. I watch
little legs churn in place
on vehement feet
which then stay glued
to the spot.
A tableau,
a moment held,
response in the balance. I watch.
In perfect choreography
little arms reach up
as bigger arms reach down:
the child is swept
into reassurance,
and silence
is immediate.

Now I have walked close enough
to search this elfin face,
to run my eyes
like caressing fingers
over its kissable skin.

I am invisible, though,
to this little being
with eyes focused elsewhere,
engrossed
in the relief of being
held.

I am partner
to this holding.
I make of us a trio—
mother, child and I,
woman stranger passing by,
who shrugged off an embryo
years ago, from whom was later
yanked a uterus
too full of fibroids
to harbor any other life.
I, woman stranger,
childless child of a mother,
connect myself into their love,
holding them
in a spirit-embrace,
joining for that moment
in their sense of
belonging,
knowing that being held
is the most perfect expression
of not being
alone
in the world.

Harbinger

> *"Is life worth leaving?"*
> — James Joyce

I.

Darkness,
and quiet.
She lies still.

Black voices
pick at her brain
like crows on carrion.

She plans to stay
wound in worthlessness,
entombed in bed linens.

She plans to take the dark fall.

Outside her window
a robin bugles breaking news:
Light to Come, Night to Open into Dawn.

She draws the sheet back
from her face and tells the robin,
"Wait, worm-eater, and I will feed you."

Wings of the deep
in their bottle on her nightstand
wait like raptors.

Darkness.
Her moment.
Now.

But the robin hawks his headlines,
ruffling the peace.
A banner of blank morning
hovers below the eastern clouds,
waiting for a story.

Could she?

II.

"Today, today, today," the robin trills,
stirring the stillness
with his urgency.

His summons flutters her thoughts
like the wings of a new bird
attempting the air.

Could she?

She unwinds the sheets
and reaches. The hollow
in the pillow

marks her flight.
She sings back,
rescued.

Greylock Bond

His stack of paper squared
in the desk drawer,

its brown sheath
torn and wrinkled
like a snakeskin
about to be shed.

How taut,
the rectangles of blue and pink
lines, the surface poised
to take his measured words.

How tense,
the authority of his hand
striding across the page
scarring the sheet beneath.

How tight,
this relic of his world,
lord over us in life,
worm-smile at us in death.

I know the code
revealed on each page
when held to the light:
"GREYLOCK BOND
An LLBROWN *paper.*"

He locked us in the bondage
of his beatings.

Here it is,
my father's stack of paper

waiting in my desk drawer,
expecting my words
like a tombstone
about to be engraved.

After Twenty Years
    after Sharon Olds

When you shuffled before me,
face blank
like someone playing poker
with worthless cards,

when you averted
your gray-blue eyes,
now gone leaden
with lack of interest,

when you edged away from me
seeking to hide
in your newspaper or your program or anything
to avoid my questions, when you mouthed
It's fine, sweetheart, our marriage is fine, the shifting
of your feet a dead give-away that you wished
yourself light-years away from my questions,
I could not
find the air to breathe
into my lungs to
keep my hope alive.

The space around you seemed to shrink,
folding in upon itself, threatening
to suck me into nowhere. I felt the urge
to dig in my heels, to pull against that pull into nothing,
to release the crushing pressure of monotony and
wail *What happened, what happened to us?* and
I wanted to shake you by your shoulders and
wrench your gaze into mine and shout into the vacuum
and hear a voice other than my own. I wanted
to yank you out of your emotional inertia, to
shine some light back into our couplehood.

But as you turned your back to me
and slowly fled the room,
my spine turned to string
and my knees turned to dust

and I wondered whether I could ever
cross that void
of you.

Sentinel
for my brother Mike, who was there

Five steps from bed to window—
you turn it into miles of back and forth,
mark-time-marching
because you just can't sit
under the wet wool blanket
of waiting.

You stay, as faithful as the question
of his love, blood
of his blood, your marching
meshed with his heartbeat,
with his beatings
as his son.

You walk and watch and walk and stay,
slipping out at last
for air and a beer
with a friend—
care for the caregiver.

He still has strength to criticize.

Twenty-three hours there
plus one hour away
equals neglect.

Nothing is good enough for Dad.

So you're there you're there you're there.
You couldn't think,
mind scraped numb by the hours.
You tried to pray though Dad said
Hail Marys didn't work anymore.

No word on the Our Father.

Five steps from bed to window,
one for each of us kids,

your throat pinching
at each turn,
watching him fail.

You tried.
You were like a puppy
wriggling at possibility,
sitting up for Dad's praise,
fetching hope like a rubber ball.

You watched and waited and watched
him frown, eyes empty as windows
of a deserted house,
searching your face
trying to place you.
"Number One Son,"
your heart still heard him say—
a prize after three girls.
You turned to the window one time—
one of hundreds of times—
turned back to the bed—
it was just an instant—
looked—
in an instant—
ran to the nurses—
"He's not breathing"—
and they, looking at you funny—
as if, what did you expect—
you looked away
once too often.

That damned window.
He slipped past you.

My Father's Hands

Thick like German sausage,
gold band on the left ring finger,
Notre Dame class ring on the right,
nails groomed to perfection,

engulfing the cup
with thumb and forefinger
while chatting with me
and my dolls over tea,

dipping fingertips
in talcum powder, hopping them
across the dining room table
around our Easter baskets,

closing around mine
like oven mitts
to dance with me
standing on his feet,

engraving his name
in black slants
of authority
on my report cards,

wielding a tennis racket,
hoisting trophies
and bourbons
at the country club,

slapping my face,
hurling lightning into my vision,
needles of hurt
into my heart,

lighting a chain
of cigarettes
as long as decades,
flicking ash and years away,

lying on his chest,
as empty as a broken promise,
arms crossed at the wrist
in the pine box,

I hold my father's hands
in my history.

When You Pray

After the horse is calm again
and the snake has crawled away
and the dust in the distance
announces medics from the ranch,

after the hospital doors have closed
and the machines have clicked
their pictures and the doctors
have seen his brain-shadow,

after the surgeons have drilled
and the blood has pooled out
and the questions have flown
from every direction,

after his dyslexia has flipped back
and his balance has normalized
and the note is on the bathroom mirror
to remind him, daily, of his name

because he must reconstruct his past
which has hit the ground with him
and fled into desert shadow
with the rattlesnake,

after the doctors have covered their aptitudes
with "Give it time" and "No guarantees"
and the vastness of loss
rears up at you,

after the hot breath
of "Oh please oh please oh please"
has ripped through the canyon
of your soul

and you've reintroduced yourself
to God saying yes,
it's been a long time,
but could we overlook that for now,

that
is when you pray,

because who are we
without our memories,

and who are you
without
his memory
of you.

What Remains of a Life

When all's said and done,
the give and take, build and break,
what mark will you leave?

Susan Blair is a poet, writer and award-winning speaker. A retired federal employee, she has also worked in sales and computer systems analysis; additionally, she has taught a variety of group exercise classes for over 20 years. She graduated *cum laude* from Middlebury College in Vermont with a BA in German and Russian (double major). In addition to Vermont, she has lived in Rhode Island, New York, New Jersey, Oklahoma, Pennsylvania, Virginia, Germany and Seattle. She currently resides in Wenatchee, Washington.

Susan also writes poetry for children. She has written a series of five poetry-activity books, which are illustrated for coloring in with discussion questions at the back.

She appears in costume as "Perri the Poetry Fairy," reading poems to elementary school children.

www.ingramcontent.com/pod-product-compliance
Lightning Source LLC
LaVergne TN
LVHW041518070426
835507LV00012B/1656